Original title:

Velveteen Hats Under the Elf Stud

Author: Kätriin Kaldaru

ISBN HARDBACK: 978-1-80563-030-2

ISBN PAPERBACK: 978-1-80564-551-1

Delight in the Swaying Branches

In the whispering woods, branches sway,
Painting the air in a dance of play.
Sunlight filters through leaves so green,
Nature's embrace, a tranquil scene.

Songs of the birds echo sweet and clear,
Each note a story, each melody dear.
With every rustle, the secrets confide,
In the heart of the trees, where wonders abide.

A Glimpse of Fabricated Fantasies

In the realm where dreams softly weave,
Imagination blooms, and hearts believe.
Castle walls shimmer with magic's glow,
Adventures await in the stories we sow.

Through portals of fairy tales, we glide,
Where unicorns prance and the brave confide.
Moments of wonder, so vividly spun,
In a world of enchantment, we're never undone.

Threads of Solitude and Laughter

In the quiet corners, shadows reside,
Silence wraps warmly, a gentle guide.
Laughter lingers, a spark in the night,
Filling the void with whispers of light.

Solitude dances with joy intertwined,
Echoes of memories, sweetly aligned.
Through threads of the past, they twirl and sway,
Weaving a tapestry of yesterday.

Hats That Speak to the Heart of Enchantment

Upon the shelf, they sit with grace,
Hats of charm in every place.
Whimsical brims and colors so bright,
Each telling tales in the soft moonlight.

With a flick of the wrist, a spell is cast,
Mysteries hidden in stitches so vast.
Oh, the dreams that they weave in the night,
Hats that whisper to hearts in flight.

The Playful Caps of Nature's Masquerade

In twilight's charm, the mushrooms gleam,
With polka dots as if from a dream.
They dance in circles on the soft moss bed,
Whispering secrets that the forest bred.

A cap of crimson with golden trim,
Underneath whispers of the moon's whim.
They twirl beneath the leaves so spry,
Nature's jesters in a night sky high.

With laughter caught in the breezy sighs,
The woodland's cheer as the day slowly dies.
In playful harmony, they rise and fall,
Their vibrant caps enchanting all.

Some mimic fairies, some act the fool,
Each one a master of nature's school.
In the hush of night, a radiant spread,
Of colors bright, where dreams are fed.

So join the dance, let your spirit soar,
Through nature's masquerade, forevermore.
For in its whimsy, we find our part,
The caps of joy, a wild, sweet heart.

Elven Artistry Beneath Starlit Canopies

Beneath the boughs where shadows play,
Elven hands weave night from day.
With silken threads of silver light,
They stitch the stars into the night.

A symphony of whispers shared,
In glades where magic's gently aired.
Their artistry in moonlit bloom,
Paints the darkness with sweet perfume.

With brush of time, they draw the sky,
Each sparkle placed with a painter's sigh.
The constellations bow with grace,
To the elven touch in this sacred space.

As twilight wraps the world in dreams,
Their laughter echoes by silver streams.
In dances spun of starlit grace,
Elven artistry finds its place.

So wander lost where the shadows blend,
In secret woods where wonders extend.
For under canopies where spirits roam,
The elven heart shall call you home.

Tints and Colors of Whimsy

In the garden of dreams, colors play,
Hues of laughter chase the gray,
Brushes dipped in magic bright,
Painting daydreams in the light.

With a flick of a wrist, skies turn blue,
Sunsets shimmer in vibrant hue,
Whispers of wonder in every shade,
The heart's secrets are artfully laid.

Around every corner, joy bursts forth,
In the tints of mirth, we find our worth,
Glimmers of hope in pastel skies,
Where imagination learns to rise.

A touch of gold, a sprinkle of green,
In the world of whimsy, so much unseen,
Each color a story waiting to bloom,
In the tapestry woven, banishing gloom.

So dance in the colors, let laughter reign,
In the shades of delight, forget the pain,
For every heartbeat beats in time,
With the vibrant echoes of life's sweet rhyme.

Tails Woven in Starry English

Beneath the stars, tales come alive,
Whiskered companions, brave and sly,
Each tale stitched in cosmic thread,
With laughter shared and dreams spread.

Moonlit paths where secrets lie,
Tails intertwine with a gentle sigh,
In the hush of night, they find their way,
Through the whispers of dusk till break of day.

In the glint of eyes, mischief stirs,
As words dance light in soft-furred furs,
Stories weave like the night's embrace,
Binding our souls in a starry lace.

A comet's tail, a flicker, a flash,
Moments in time come together, a splash,
Each dreamer hopes for the night to unfold,
In the language of starlight, stories told.

So gather the tails that twirl and spin,
In the fabric of night, let the adventures begin,
For in this vast cosmos, there's space for us all,
In the wonder of tales, we rise and we fall.

Creatures of Fabric in Twilight

In the twilight glow, fabric stirs,
Creatures emerge, soft as purrs,
Stitched from moonlight and dreams profound,
In this quiet hour, magic is found.

A bear of velvet, a fox of thread,
Adventures await where imagination's led,
In pockets of twilight, they whisper and weave,
Tales on the wind for those who believe.

With buttons for eyes and hearts made of fluff,
Each creature knows when the world's been tough,
So they kindle the spark, in shadows they play,
Bring warmth and comfort to close of day.

They dart through the fabric, both vibrant and bright,
Woven as one in the fabric of night,
In the patchwork of dreams, their spirits take flight,
Bringing joy to the hearts that hold them tight.

These creatures of fabric will always belong,
In the twilight of wonder, they sing their song,
So gather them close, let your heart take the lead,
For in every stitch, there blooms a new need.

The Enchanted Needle and the Forest

In the heart of the forest, a needle gleams,
With magic threaded through silken dreams,
A wand of creation, with every stitch,
Crafting the wonders of a woodland rich.

The trees hold secrets in whispering shrouds,
As creatures marvel amidst leafy crowds,
With each tiny stitch, a new tale is spun,
In the embrace of nature, stories run.

A tapestry woven of laughter and light,
Embracing the shadows that dance in the night,
The needle hums softly, the fabric does sigh,
As a chorus of wonders begins to fly.

Through meadows and glades, the whimsy awakes,
In the magic of making, the silence breaks,
With each twist and turn of the enchanted thread,
The forest comes alive, as dreams are fed.

So wander the woods with an open heart,
For the enchanted needle plays its part,
In every creation of fabric and lore,
Awaits a magic we simply adore.

Tails of Tapestry and Whimsy

In a world where shadows play,
Threads of gold in bright array,
Each tale weaves through night and day,
Magic lingers, come what may.

Whispers dance in colors bold,
Dreams are spun from silk and gold,
Every stitch a secret told,
In this fabric dreams unfold.

Knots of laughter, knots of fear,
Adventures call, our hearts sincere,
From each corner, joy draws near,
In the tapestry, we revere.

With a flick, the stories rise,
Swirling soft like evening skies,
Each twist a spark, a sweet surprise,
In the loom where magic lies.

So gather 'round, both young and old,
In this woven tale retold,
Every heart a thread of gold,
In the whimsy, life unfolds.

Hidden Adornments in the Mist

Veiled in fog, a treasure's gleam,
Whispers float, like half a dream,
Secrets hidden, lost in theme,
A world where magic's not extreme.

Softly woven in the air,
Glimmers twinkle, unaware,
In the silence, tales laid bare,
Hidden adornments everywhere.

Beneath the weeping willow's sway,
Glimmers pulse where fairies play,
Each droplet, like a star's ballet,
In the dusk, twilight takes away.

Paths entwine where shadows loom,
Mysteries pulse, like flowers bloom,
In the heart, a quiet room,
Spoils of wonder start to plume.

Beyond the mist, a soft refrain,
In each heart, the quiet gain,
For treasures found are not in vain,
In the hidden, life is plain.

Celestial Threads of Imagination

In the night where stars ignite,
Dreams take flight in softest light,
Threads of wonder soar in sight,
Weaving worlds by heart's delight.

Nebulas paint the sky so deep,
Cosmic tales that never sleep,
Galaxies in shadows creep,
Through the darkness, secrets leap.

Crickets sing their midnight song,
In the throng where dreams belong,
Every note a magic strong,
In this dance, we all belong.

From the earth, we reach for grace,
With our minds, we map this space,
In the stars, we find our place,
Celestial threads we now embrace.

So hold your hopes like precious seeds,
Tend to them with gentle deeds,
In the night, the heart still leads,
To the cosmos where joy feeds.

Hats of Harmony and Enchantment

Upon our heads, in colors bright,
Hats of wonder, pure delight,
With each wearer, dreams take flight,
In the day and through the night.

Every brim holds secrets tight,
Spun from laughter, hope, and light,
In a world where all is right,
Harmony sings, an endless sight.

Some are tall, and some are wide,
With every stitch, our hearts confide,
In this journey, side by side,
Worn with love, our spirits glide.

When the clouds begin to part,
Wear your hat, a work of art,
For in our heads, we play our part,
In each heartbeat, dreams impart.

So tip your hat to all you see,
In this realm of fantasy,
For through the hats, we find the key,
To a life that's wild and free.

The Tapestry of Enigma

In shadows deep, where whispers play,
Threads of fate begin to sway.
A tapestry spun with secrets tight,
Woven in the loom of night.

Colors dance in shades of grey,
Mysteries beckon, come what may.
Each stitch a tale, each knot a dream,
A world unfurls, a silver seam.

Entwined in fate, the figures twirl,
Their stories twist, a mystic swirl.
In every fold, a truth to find,
A spark ignites, the heart entwined.

Glimmers shine through threads of dust,
In beauty's bind, we place our trust.
The loom of life, a wondrous sight,
Where day meets night, and wrong meets right.

So take a step, let wonder lead,
In the tapestry, plant your seed.
For in its weave, your tale is spun,
Embrace the enigma, let dreams run.

Glistening Dreams in Shadowed Woods

In shadowed woods where whispers sigh,
The trees hold secrets, ancient nigh.
Glistening dreams in moonlit streams,
Awake the heart, unleash the dreams.

Beneath the boughs, the stories creep,
In silver light, the spirits leap.
Each rustling leaf, a voice of lore,
A gentle call from times before.

Mystic shadows weave their grace,
In every corner, a hidden place.
With every step, the echoes blend,
A journey where the path transcends.

The twilight hum, a lullaby,
As fireflies flicker, dance and fly.
In gossamer dreams, the night is spun,
And deep in woods, all hearts are one.

So wander through, let marvels rise,
In shadowed woods, beneath the skies.
For glistening dreams await in trees,
A promise made on whispered breeze.

Mysteries Woven in Moonlight

Beneath the moon, where secrets flow,
Mysteries weave their silver glow.
A fabric of night, so soft and grand,
Threads of wonder, spun by hand.

In silence deep, the stars confide,
In whispered tones, they cannot hide.
Each pattern tells of times gone by,
A story wrapped in night's soft sigh.

The moonlit path, a guiding thread,
In woven dreams, we dare to tread.
With every step, the heart beats wild,
In hushed embrace, we're nature's child.

So gather close, embrace the night,
For mysteries bloom in soft moonlight.
In threads unseen, our fates align,
A binding bond, eternally twine.

For in this sphere, our worlds combine,
To share a dance, a secret sign.
We weave together with whispered grace,
In moonlit realms, we find our place.

Caps of Wonder and Mystique

In the market square, where wonders grow,
Caps of mystique in vibrant row.
Each hat a tale, some bold, some sly,
Whispers of magic beneath the sky.

With feathers bright and colors grand,
Each woven stitch, a wizard's hand.
Choices to don, both strange and rare,
In caps of wonder, adventures dare.

The pointed peak, a sorcerer's pride,
In velvet soft, let dreams abide.
Cloaked in charms, in laughter's clutch,
The world awakens with a gentle touch.

Beneath the brim, the secrets hide,
Imagination's spark, our rampant guide.
So wear a cap, embark to see,
Where wonder waits, eternally free.

For in each cap, a life to weave,
In colors bright, we dare believe.
With every glance, let visions thrive,
In caps of wonder, our dreams alive.

Secrets Worn Under Celestial Light

Beneath the moon's soft, silvery glow,
A tapestry of dreams begins to flow.
Hidden whispers twirl with the night,
Secrets worn under celestial light.

In shadows where the starlight drapes,
The gentle breeze hums tales of capes.
Each twinkle holds a story, dear,
A treasure chest of hope and fear.

For in the velvet darkness lies,
The laughter of the skies as it sighs.
Mysteries dance on the lips of trees,
Carried far by the midnight breeze.

With every heartbeat, magic spins,
In quiet corners where wonder begins.
The universe watches with eyes so bright,
As secrets bloom under the celestial light.

Oh, the fragile strands of fate entwine,
In the glimmer where the worlds align.
Come gather 'round and listen, tonight,
To secrets worn under celestial light.

Adornments of the Silhouette Dance

In the realm where shadows start to play,
Silhouettes dance as the sun slips away.
Adornments glimmer in twilight's embrace,
A balletic art, a poem of grace.

The twirl of figures sends whispers around,
Each twinkling glance a soft, secret sound.
Draped in starlight, each movement refined,
The essence of beauty, ethereal, blind.

With crescent moons piping their tune,
The night laces dreams beneath a silvered rune.
Each sway and step, a tale to be told,
Of passions ignited and hearts made bold.

As shadows expand, let your spirit glide,
Flow with the rhythm, let wishes collide.
A tapestry woven in dusk's warm hues,
Adornments of magic that none can refuse.

So join the dance, in this fairytale night,
Lose yourself in the wonder, take flight.
For in this waltz, life's mysteries enhance,
Adornments shine brightly in the silhouette dance.

Whimsical Threads of Sable Night

As twilight weaves its gentle spell,
In whispers, night begins to swell.
With starlit threads stitched tight and bright,
A cloak of dreams, a sable night.

Through tangled woods where secrets creep,
The shadows gather, the world asleep.
Each moment sparkles like a lost delight,
In whimsical threads of sable night.

The moon, a lantern, hangs on high,
Illuminating paths where wishes fly.
Veils of laughter float on the air,
With echoes of magic, sweet and rare.

In corners where enchanted sighs reside,
The world is cloaked; let dreams be your guide.
For within the darkness, hope takes flight,
In whimsical threads of sable night.

So embrace the wonders that shadows glean,
Let your heart dance in scenes unseen.
For in the quiet, joy will ignite,
With whimsical threads of sable night.

Stitches of Sonorous Echoes

In the fabric of night, sounds intertwine,
Each note a stitch, with purpose, divine.
Resonant chords in the evening's embrace,
Stitches of echoes weave time and space.

Through velvet whispers, the stories unfold,
Of hearts that gather, of dreams retold.
In every murmur, a heartbeat flows,
A tapestry woven where each echo glows.

The rustle of leaves, a soft serenade,
A symphony sung in the twilight's shade.
With every sigh, we share in the flow,
Stitches of sonorous echoes bestow.

So close your eyes as the melodies soar,
Let your spirit wander, let it explore.
For in the night, magic's song is bright,
In stitches of echoes, lost in the light.

Together we'll dance with notes set free,
A harmony spun through the leaves of the tree.
Come listen closely, where time starts to slow,
To stitches of sonorous echoes we'll go.

Chronicles of Starlight Stitching

In twilight's hush, the threads unravel,
Patterns dance where dreams do travel.
Sparkling hues of silver gleam,
Weaving wishes, stitching dreams.

With every knot, a tale unfolds,
Of heroes brave and hearts of gold.
Beneath the moon, each stitch will shine,
Crafting magic, divine design.

A tapestry of dusk and dawn,
In every fiber, hope is drawn.
The stars above lend light and grace,
As fate's soft hands begin to trace.

Whispers twine in shadows deep,
Secrets shared that time will keep.
In every patch, a memory spun,
In every seam, a battle won.

Thus, starlit threads entwined with care,
Bring forth the dreams that linger there.
An endless tale, forever spun,
In starlight's grasp, our hearts now run.

The Art of Crafting Dreams

With needle poised and fabric spread,
Imagination's path is tread.
Every stitch a wish, a flight,
Weaving wonder into the night.

In quiet corners, visions bloom,
Softly lit by the glow of loom.
Colors whisper of distant lands,
With hopeful threads held in our hands.

A swirl of magic shapes the air,
Each design holds tales so rare.
The fabric speaks with voices clear,
Unfolding dreams that draw us near.

As twilight drapes its velvet cloak,
The heart ignites, the spirit woke.
In craft's embrace, we find our way,
In every seam, new dreams will sway.

Thus, let the loom of life entwine,
Your spirit marked by every line.
In fabric's warmth, our hopes take flight,
As dawn again awakens light.

Splendid Shadows of Faerie Dreams

In forests deep where shadows play,
Whispers weave through night and day.
With every flicker, magic glows,
Where gentle winds of wonder blow.

The fae take flight on silken threads,
To spin their dreams in twilight's beds.
Soft laughter echoes through the trees,
As secrets dance upon the breeze.

In moonlit glades, their stories show,
Through woven boughs where moonbeams flow.
In splendid hues of twilight's sway,
The faerie dreams shall never fray.

Each shadow spins a tale anew,
Of brave desires and love so true.
In fairy rings where wishes gleam,
The heart discovers how to dream.

So close your eyes and let them roam,
In every shadow, find your home.
For in the night, with stars aglow,
A world of dreams begins to grow.

The Subtle Enchantment of Fable Hats

Upon the shelf, the fable hats,
Adorned with tales of whims and spats.
Each stitch holds stories of the bold,
In fibers soft, the dreams enfold.

A rabbit's ear, a wizard's crown,
A secret woven, a soft renown.
These hats may spark the inner flame,
Transforming hearts and lives the same.

With every wear, a magic spun,
To cloak the world in tales begun.
In colors deep or patterns bright,
They conjure wonders, day and night.

So don a hat, embrace the lore,
Adventure waits behind the door.
For in the fabric, dreams reside,
A journey sparked, a magic guide.

Thus, wear your fables with delight,
In every style, a new take flight.
For with a hat, the world will see,
The subtle threads of destiny.

The Dance of Faery Tails

In the glade where moonbeams play,
Whispers of the night in sway,
Faeries twirl on gossamer wings,
Painting dreams in silver strings.

From the flowers, a soft glow,
Light as mist, they dance and flow,
Echoes of laughter fill the air,
Magic weaves through shadows rare.

Underneath the ancient oak,
Secrets wrapped in softest cloak,
Spirits spin with twinkling grace,
In a world of sweet embrace.

Every flicker, every glance,
Summons forth a silent dance,
Where the heart can leap and soar,
And find joy forevermore.

As the dawn begins to creep,
Faery tales drift off to sleep,
Yet in dreams, they softly glide,
In the night where joys abide.

In the Realm of Starlit Stitchery

Threads of silver, needles bright,
Sewing patterns through the night,
Under stars, the fabric flows,
Tales of magic gently grows.

In the quiet, whispers hum,
Patterns dance and shadows come,
Every stitch a wish fulfilled,
In the realm where time is stilled.

Colors blend like dreams untold,
Warmth of friendships stitched in gold,
Laughter weaves through every seam,
Binding hearts in one sweet dream.

Beneath the moon's enchanting gaze,
Weaving stories all ablaze,
In the fabric of the night,
Bound together in pure light.

As the dawn begins to break,
Hope from every thread we make,
In this realm where dreams can soar,
Stitched with love forevermore.

Night's Cloak of Soft Delights

Night descends with velvet grace,
Wrapping all in dark embrace,
Stars like jewels shine above,
Whispers fill the air with love.

In the shadows, secrets keep,
Softly woven, tender sleep,
Crickets sing their lullaby,
Underneath the painted sky.

Gentle breezes kiss the trees,
Carrying sweet symphonies,
Nature's song, a soft caress,
In the quiet, hearts are blessed.

Each moment drifts like a dream,
In the moonlight's tender beam,
Night embraces every sigh,
Underneath the vast, deep sky.

As the stars begin to fade,
In the dawn, the cloak is laid,
Yet the soft delights remain,
In the heart, like gentle rain.

Lunaria's Embrace in the Woods

In the woods where shadows play,
Lunaria whispers night away,
Silver leaves in moonlight shine,
Casting spells on hearts divine.

Beneath the boughs, where secrets twine,
Nature's magic, pure and fine,
Gentle echoes voice the trees,
Carried softly on the breeze.

In this haven, dreams take flight,
Wrapped in warmth of soft moonlight,
Every heart finds solace here,
Cradled close, both far and near.

Where the wildflowers gently sway,
Tales of love forever stay,
In the embrace of tender night,
All the world feels soft and right.

As the dawn begins to break,
Lunaria sings for our sake,
In the woods, we'll find our way,
Guided by the light of day.

Adorned by Dreams of the Glade

In glades where sunlight softly plays,
Fairies dance through golden rays.
With laughter sweet, the flowers bloom,
Awakening joy, dispelling gloom.

A whisper of wind beneath the trees,
Tells tales of secrets on the breeze.
Each rustling leaf a song to share,
A symphony of magic, light as air.

Amid the ferns, where shadows blend,
The spirits gather, old as time, my friend.
They twirl and spin in twilight's gleam,
Adorned by dreams, lost in a dream.

With every breath, the glade confides,
Its wonders vast as the water tides.
So pause a while, let heart take flight,
In the jeweled arms of soft twilight.

For in this haven, pure and bright,
The glade reveals its hidden light.
Adorned by visions, forever blessed,
We find our peace, our truest rest.

Secrets in the Weaving Shadows

In whispers hushed, the shadows weave,
Tales of wonder, we scarcely believe.
A tapestry of dreams long spun,
Where secrets lie, and journeys begun.

Each flicker and fade hides a story,
A glimmer of magic, shared in glory.
The moonlight dances across the floor,
Inviting us to discover more.

With every thread, a promise made,
In midnight hues, fears gently laid.
These woven shadows, soft and deep,
Guard the dreams that we wish to keep.

As twilight calls with its gentle sigh,
The world transforms with a silver nigh.
In every silence, a heartbeat found,
In mystery's grasp, we are spellbound.

So linger here, let moments blend,
In secrets shared, a lover's mend.
For shadows have stories, waiting to tell,
In this woven world where we dwell.

The Magic of Woolen Whispers

In cozy corners, where warmth abounds,
Woolen whispers dance, in soft, rounded sounds.
Each thread a story, lovingly spun,
Binding hearts, as the yarns run.

From humble sheep, the fibers flow,
Crafted in hands, with care they grow.
In gentle stitches, love is poured,
A tapestry woven, a bond restored.

Feel the magic in each fiber tight,
As hands work wonders, from day to night.
Each project a journey, a tale of grace,
With every loop, we find our place.

The whispers of wool, they softly call,
Embracing us gently, cradling all.
In every purl, there's laughter shared,
In moments of peace, our souls are bared.

So gather your yarns, let dreams take flight,
In this magic of wool, our spirits ignite.
For in every stitch, a memory stays,
A warmth that guides us through all our days.

Enchanted Fabrics of Luminous Drifting

In realms where starlight weaves the night,
Enchanted fabrics shimmer bright.
Patterns dance in silken grace,
A world of wonder, a sacred space.

Each bolt of cloth, a wish unspun,
Threads entwined, two souls become one.
With every fold, a dream emerges,
In luminous drifting, magic surges.

The colors sing as moonbeams trace,
A delicate touch, a warm embrace.
Through shimmering layers, secrets roam,
In the heart of the fabric, we find our home.

With every drape, a story flows,
Unraveling mysteries only fabric knows.
In the quilt of night, where shadows merge,
Enchanted we live, as dreams emerge.

So let the fabrics wrap us tight,
In luminous drifting, through the night.
For within each thread, our hopes reside,
In this tapestry woven, side by side.

Echoes of the Woven Sky

In the twilight's gentle hue,
Stars begin their dance anew.
Whispers rise from earth to air,
Dreams entwined, a lovers' snare.

Clouds like threads across the night,
Weaving tales of pure delight.
With every twinkle, shadows play,
In the echoes, worlds sway.

Beneath this vast and open dome,
Hearts take flight, forever roam.
Each sigh a note, each wish a year,
Together, hopes resound so near.

Night's embrace, a lullaby,
Cradled softly, we comply.
In this wonder, lost in time,
The woven sky, a life sublime.

The Mystique of Headgear

In the attic, dust and dreams,
A hat awaits, or so it seems.
Feathers, ribbons, stories spun,
Whispers of old, adventures begun.

Straw and silk, a crown of grace,
Worn by many, none can trace.
Every fold a memory holds,
Of laughter, secrets, myths untold.

This headgear speaks of days long past,
Of gentle winds and shadows cast.
Each stitch a heartbeat, each seam a thread,
In the mystique where dreams are fed.

Turn it gently, lift with care,
Ghosts of wearers linger there.
In its brim, the world aligns,
Eager hearts, enchanted minds.

Glistening Hues Beneath the Canopy

In the forest, whispers breathe,
Glistening hues beneath the leaves.
Emerald dreams on branches high,
Painting secrets in the sky.

Sunlight dances, shadows flick,
Nature's brush, a gentle trick.
Each leaf a note, each petal spins,
A symphony where life begins.

Twilight spills its golden ink,
Painting moments in a blink.
From blooms of violet to gold of sun,
Beneath the canopy, magic's spun.

Here the faeries weave their tales,
As the moonlight softly pales.
In the hush, in the still,
Glistening hues, a heart to fill.

The Dance of the Nightly Tailor

Under stars, the shadows hum,
A nightly tailor's work begun.
With silver threads and moonlit spools,
He crafts enchantments, breaking rules.

Each stitch a tale of lost desire,
Wrapped in dreams that never tire.
With nimble fingers, patterns weave,
In darkness spun, the heart believes.

Around him twirl the whispered mist,
No moment lost, no chance to resist.
In the pauses, feathers light,
A dance that plays throughout the night.

When dawn arrives with blushing grace,
Nightly threads slow their pace.
Yet in the morning's golden beam,
The tailor's magic haunts the dream.

A Tapestry of Fables

In the heart of a forest, tales entwine,
Whispers of magic, both ancient and fine.
Creatures of wonder, in shadows they play,
Every rustle a story, come dance in the sway.

The owls tell secrets, the stars keep their watch,
Each flicker of light, a memorable notch.
Bound by enchantment, the night softly sighs,
In the weave of the fables, true beauty lies.

A brook babbles softly, a chorus so sweet,
Echoing laughter where dreamers hearts meet.
The tapestry stretches, both wide and profound,
In its intricate threads, our hearts will be found.

Misty illusions sway with the breeze,
In their soft embrace, we find gentle ease.
Every fiber a memory, woven so tight,
This tapestry beckons, a call in the night.

So gather your dreams, let them soar and take flight,
In the depths of this forest, a world of pure light.
For within every fable, a truth waits to gleam,
In the heart of the night, we are free to dream.

Twinkling Beacons in the Night

Stars twinkle softly, like whispers of old,
Beacons of magic, in stories retold.
Each glimmer a promise, a wish in the sky,
A dance of enchantment, where dreams learn to fly.

The moon weaves its silver, a cloak for the dark,
Painting the heavens, igniting a spark.
With every soft shimmer, a path starts to gleam,
Guiding each wanderer, igniting their dream.

In the depths of the night, secrets unfurl,
Each twinkling beacon, a bright, shining pearl.
They beckon the weary, the lost, and the brave,
With stories of courage, the heart they will save.

As comets race by, trailing light in their wake,
New journeys are born, the night's magic at stake.
A canvas unfolds, adorned with delight,
Twinkling beacons in the depth of the night.

So look to the sky, let your soul take flight,
For dreams are ignited in twinkling starlight.
Find solace in shadows, let worries take flight,
Embrace the enchantment of the magical night.

The Glistening Charm of Midnight Fabric

Midnight fabric, woven from dreams,
Glistening softly, reflecting moonbeams.
Threads of silver, each story they weave,
In the still of the night, we learn to believe.

A tapestry spun with the hopes of the stars,
Each stitch a reminder that magic is ours.
In the hush of the evening, where shadows will play,
The charm of the fabric will guide our way.

With every shimmer, a wish in the dark,
Illuminating whispers that set off a spark.
The midnight allure, so delicate and right,
Wrap us in layers of soft, comforting light.

A canvas of silence, where dreams intertwine,
Echoes of laughter in each sacred line.
In this fabric of midnight, we find who we are,
With shimmering threads, we gather and spar.

So linger a moment in wonders we share,
Find solace and peace in this gentle affair.
The glistening charm of this fabric, our guide,
As we journey together, hearts open wide.

Starlit Crowns and Mystic Weaves

A crown made of starlight rests on the night,
With diamonds and dreams, a truly grand sight.
Mystic weaves twirl in a dance so divine,
Where shadows and sparkles in harmony shine.

Each thread holds a secret, a wish to be known,
As wisdom of ages through time has been sewn.
In the heart of the starlit, where echoes may roam,
We weave our own magic, we craft our own home.

The night sings a lullaby, gentle and low,
While the crown of the cosmos begins to bestow.
A blessing of calm wrapped in silvery grace,
A soft, tender moment, a warm, sweet embrace.

Lift your eyes to the heavens, let dreams fill your mind,
In starlit crowns woven, a treasure to find.
With mystic weaves calling, our spirits take flight,
In the embrace of the stars, we lose the night's fright.

So come, hold your breath as the magic unfolds,
With each woven story, a promise retold.
In the glow of the starlight, our souls intertwine,
With starlit crowns shining, our hearts truly shine.

Matrices of Magic and Tailoring

In twilight's weave, the threads entwine,
Through spell and stitch, a tale divine.
Patterns shift, in whispers soft,
With needles sharp, our dreams aloft.

Colors dance, like stars on high,
Each fabric breathes a secret sigh.
From hands that craft with artful glee,
A whispered wish, a blessed decree.

Wands are raised with utmost care,
In needle's eye, the magic's lair.
With every knot and turn aligned,
A world unfolds, enchanted, kind.

The seamstress hums a haunting tune,
Awakening shadows beneath the moon.
Fragments of dreams and wishes spun,
Threads of tomorrow have just begun.

In matrices both bold and bright,
Each garment holds a spark of light.
With every cloak and every gown,
Our stories weave, as magic's crown.

Tinted Dreams Beneath the Arched Heights

Under arches where shadows play,
Tinted dreams drift and sway.
Whispers of wishes fill the air,
In a world spun fine as silk and rare.

Colors burst like laughter's sound,
In every corner, charm is found.
Glimmers of hope through glass so bright,
Casting rainbows in the fading light.

With each heartbeat, the night unfolds,
Stories of starfire, softly told.
Underneath the vast, starlit dome,
Each dream takes flight, a wayward home.

Through tales of joy and shades of pain,
Life's rich tapestry weaves its gain.
Dancing shadows, a celestial flight,
Tinted dreams set the heart alight.

Embrace the magic, the night's embrace,
Beneath the arches, time finds its place.
In every color, in every gleam,
Lies the pulse of a timeless dream.

Enchanted Millinery of the Wayward Wind

In a shop of hats where wishes bloom,
Each crown of lace dispels the gloom.
With feathers bright and fabric fine,
Every creation, a story divine.

The wayward wind wraps 'round and weaves,
Tales of adventure in the leaves.
Every turn of the breeze will find,
A hat that speaks to the wandering mind.

From wide-brimmed dreams to caps of charm,
Each piece adorned with magic's arm.
Whispers of journeys, echoes of glee,
The milliner's art—wild and free.

Under the awning, the world awaits,
Each hat a portal to untold fates.
Crowning glory in sunlight's gleam,
A dance of shadows, a waking dream.

In feathers soft and ribbons bright,
The wind sings secrets, takes to flight.
With every hat, a tale unfolds,
In enchanted ways, the magic molds.

Trees Wearing Secrets

In the forest deep where shadows creep,
Tall trees stand, their secrets keep.
Bark like pages, stories untold,
Whispers of ages in branches old.

Roots entwined with the earth's embrace,
Holding memories in time and space.
Leaves that rustle with tales of yore,
Echoing dreams from the forest floor.

Beneath the canopy, sunlight glows,
Casting patterns like nature's prose.
Each ring a chapter, a life well-lived,
In every tree, a heart that's given.

In the twilight hour, secrets thrum,
With every breeze, the ancestors hum.
A dance of shadows, a symphony,
Trees whispering truths for all to see.

Guardians old of the land they stand,
Holding wisdom, both strong and grand.
In their embrace, our spirits soar,
Trees wear their secrets forevermore.

Echoes of Softness in Nature's Grasp

In whispered tones, the leaves do sigh,
Beneath the touch of a gentle sky.
The babbling brook with secrets told,
Cradles dreams that never grow old.

Soft petals dance in twilight's glow,
And shadows weave where soft winds blow.
Each creature speaks, a tale to share,
Of love and loss, of hope laid bare.

The moonlight drapes a silken shawl,
A glowing quilt that warms us all.
In every rustle, each faint sigh,
Nature's heartbeats fluttering by.

A tapestry of colors bright,
Awakens wonder in the night.
With every sound, a story spins,
In harmony, where life begins.

The Craft of Nightly Allure

When darkness falls, the stars ignite,
Their shimmering threads of pure delight.
The moon, a beacon in velvet skies,
Calls forth the dreams that never die.

The nightingale sings a wistful tune,
Beneath the watchful gaze of the moon.
Her melodies weave through shadowed wood,
Where echoes dance, and silence stood.

Crickets join in a gentle choir,
Stirring hearts with their soft desire.
In the hush, secrets dare to rise,
As night unfolds her mystery guise.

Stars twinkle like wishes in flight,
Illuminating the vast, dark night.
Every glance reveals magic unseen,
In the craft of night's endless sheen.

Woven Tales at Dusk's Embrace

In dusky realms, where shadows play,
The sun bids farewell to the day.
Colors blend, a painter's hand,
Crafting dreams upon the land.

A breeze carries whispers from afar,
Bringing stories written in a star.
Each leaf holds a memory's trace,
Of joyous laughter, a tender face.

Beneath the arch of twilight's glow,
Secrets linger where whispers flow.
The night takes hold in gentle grace,
Embracing all in its warm embrace.

As crickets strum their evening hymn,
The world drifts into shadows dim.
Woven tales in dusk's sweet hold,
Unravel stories waiting to be told.

The Charm of Woven Ephemera

In delicate strands, the past entwines,
As fleeting moments weave through time.
Each memory, a fragile thread,
A tapestry of words unsaid.

The morning dew on petals bright,
Glitters softly in the light.
Nature's charm, a fleeting glance,
Provokes the heart to dream and dance.

With every breath, a story's spun,
Of laughter shared, of battles won.
In every shadow, every spark,
Lie hidden tales within the dark.

Ephemeral whispers on the breeze,
Tell of love that puts the heart at ease.
Our lives, a quilt of joys and tears,
Embracing both our hopes and fears.

Tales from the Enchanted Meadow

In the meadow where the daisies sway,
Whispers of magic dance and play.
Beneath the sun's warm, golden beams,
Dreamers awaken to secret dreams.

A silver brook that twinkles bright,
Reflects the stars in the velvet night.
Glowing fairies with laughter light,
Guide lost hearts with their gentle flight.

Each flower blooms with a soft, sweet song,
Where weary souls can truly belong.
In the air, a promise hangs above,
Of friendship, joy, and gentle love.

Through rolling hills and ancient trees,
The whispers of history ride the breeze.
Every step taken, a story unfolds,
In the enchanted meadow where time holds.

So come, dear friend, and linger here,
With magic woven in every sphere.
For in this space, you'll find your part,
Tales from a meadow that holds the heart.

Hat of Dreams and Fey Reflections

In a cupboard, old and filled with dust,
A hat lies waiting, wrapped in trust.
With a flicker of light and a whisper of fate,
It opens the door to dreams so great.

Beneath its brim, worlds spin and swirl,
Magic threads weave, a silken pearl.
Each night's wish takes on a new disguise,
As the fey reflections laugh and rise.

When morning comes, dreams fade away,
Yet memories linger, bright as day.
Each soft whisper in the hat's embrace,
Reveals lost hopes that time can trace.

So wear it proud, dear seeker of lore,
For within its depths, there lies more.
A hat of dreams, a fey delight,
To guide you gently through the night.

Dance with the shadows, chase the light,
With every dream, take bold flight.
For in every stitch, there lies a tale,
Of fey reflections along the trail.

The Sway of Shadowed Embellishments

In the twilight's hush, shadows creep,
Whispers of secrets in silence sleep.
Flickering candlelight casts strange forms,
As the night air softly warms.

Embellished tales that flicker and sway,
Unravel the fabric of endearing gray.
A tapestry woven with threads of night,
In the dance of shadows, find your light.

Fragments of laughter echo through time,
In the whispering woods, a gentle rhyme.
Every rustle, a soft-spoken truth,
That proves the magic of joy and youth.

In the moon's embrace, all shadows blend,
Each twist and turn, a tale without end.
As the night weaves its intricate dance,
We find ourselves lost in a sweet chance.

So listen closely, keep your heart wide,
For in shadowed embellishments, dreams reside.
Every heartbeat, a call to explore,
The magic that lives just beyond the door.

Silken Secrets in the Glade

In the glade where silence sings,
Lies a treasure of forgotten things.
Silken secrets wrap around trees,
Carried softly by the gentle breeze.

Beneath the boughs where moonlight drips,
Nature's voice in sweet whispers slips.
And with each step, a tale unfurls,
Of magic woven in silken swirls.

The soft glow of fireflies takes flight,
Illuminating stories written in light.
Longing eyes seek what's pure and true,
As the glade reveals what's meant for you.

Crickets sing a lullaby near,
To calm the heart and soothe the fear.
In this stillness, wisdom breathes,
As ancient roots weave among the leaves.

So linger on, embrace the night,
Where silken secrets spark delight.
For in the glade, mysteries unfold,
In whispers soft and tales retold.

Crafting Night's Silhouette

In twilight's cloak, the shadows grow,
A whispering wind, a lull to bestow.
The stars are sewn in the fabric of dreams,
Where magic dances in moonlit beams.

On cobbled paths of silver and mist,
The night reveals its enchanting twist.
With every stitch, the hour unveils,
A symphony sung by the nightingale's tales.

The darkness hums with secrets untold,
While shimmering silks of starlight unfold.
In the heart of night, a tapestry spun,
By hands that weave magic, till night is done.

Glimmers of hope in the quiet breathe,
Each thread a promise, joy to bequeath.
So gather the dreams that the night has sown,
And wear them brightly, for you are not alone.

With every heartbeat, the night unfolds,
A canvas painted in whispers of gold.
In the shadows where magic reigns,
Embrace the beauty that softly remains.

The Allure of Magic Thread

In twilight's grip, where wonders gleam,
The magic thread flows like a dream.
It spirals round in colors bold,
Tales of enchantment in hues untold.

With nimble fingers, the weavers toil,
Creating stories from midnight soil.
Each stitch a wish, each knot a sigh,
Binding the earth to the star-speckled sky.

Upon the loom of the heart's desire,
The threads ignite with a soft, warm fire.
Bringing to life the myths long lost,
In the dance of creation, not counting the cost.

The whispers of cloth, the sighs of the night,
Bring forth the magic where shadows alight.
In the fabric woven with dreams as the base,
It spells adventure, a timeless embrace.

So hold tight to the thread that weaves your fate,
For in its embrace, you shall resonate.
In the mystery spun from the dark into light,
Find your own magic, take flight on the night.

Whimsy in the Glistening Grove

In a grove where the fairies play,
Twinkling lights chase the shadows away.
Laughter bubbles in streams of delight,
As stars peek through the veil of night.

With every rustle and whisper of leaves,
The magic of mischief gently weaves.
Elusive creatures on soft, silent feet,
Invite you to join, oh, so sweet.

There's whimsy found in the dance of the breeze,
A hint of adventure in every tree.
The moon, a witness, smiles down from above,
Bestowing the grove with a blessing of love.

Curled ferns whisper secrets to the night,
While shadows shimmer in soft twilight.
Lose yourself in this enchanted place,
Where wonder and reality intertwine with grace.

So wander and weave through the glistening spires,
Let your spirit be lifted on gentle lyres.
For in this grove, magic finds your heart,
Awakening joy, a most wondrous art.

Folklore Wrapped in Spun Light

In corners dark, where stories hide,
Folklore beckons with arms open wide.
Each tale unravels like soft-spun gold,
Whispers of wisdom, both gentle and bold.

The flicker of fire draws you near,
As shadows dance and begin to appear.
From woven tales of yore, entwined,
A tapestry forms of the magic aligned.

The lightness of laughter, the weight of a fear,
All echo through time, the past drawing near.
In spinnerets of fate, strands intertwine,
Creating the legends that forever shine.

Each character crafted from dreams we recall,
In the night's embrace, we rise and we fall.
With every new thread, the past finds a home,
As long as whispers in twilight may roam.

So gather round, let the stories elate,
For in folklore wrapped, we navigate fate.
In the glow of the night, find the spark of your light,
And hold fast to the magic that thrives in our sight.

Echoes of the Midnight Tailor

In the quietude of night, soft shadows play,
A tailor whispers dreams, in stitches they lay.
Each thread a story, woven with care,
Awakening wonders, enchantments to share.

Beneath the moon's gaze, fabrics take flight,
Dancing with stars, in silken delight.
A needle's precision, a flicker of light,
Crafting the magic, hidden from sight.

With each tiny snip, a wish is set free,
A tapestry bright, stitched with glee.
Echoes of laughter, reverberate true,
In the midnight's embrace, dreams start anew.

Yet as dawn begins to unfurl its gold,
The tailor retreats, with secrets untold.
His workshop abandoned, but with threads that bind,
The echoes of magic linger behind.

For every young dreamer who chases the night,
Will find in their heart, the tailor's soft light.
In shadows of twilight, their wonders await,
As whispers of fabrics unlock every fate.

Thrumming Threads of Mirth and Magic

Through verdant valleys, where laughter resounds,
Threaded with mirth, where enchantment abounds.
A loom spins joy, where spirits convene,
Woven with giggles, in places unseen.

Golden hues dance in the amber sun,
Weaving stories together, two hearts become one.
Shimmering glances through silken soft pages,
Allowing the magic to echo through ages.

In shadows and light, the yarn entwines,
Connecting the heartstrings, weaving the signs.
Each knot tells a tale of laughter and tears,
A fabric of friendship, over the years.

So gather your dreams, let your spirits take flight,
For in every stitch, there's a glimpse of the light.
With threads made of laughter, spun from delight,
Mirth dances freely, throughout day and night.

The loom hums a tune of whimsical cheer,
As magic twirls lively, drawing us near.
With every new dawn, our hearts will ignite,
In the thrumming of threads, the world feels just right.

Secrets in the Starlit Glade

In the hush of the evening, when twilight appears,
Secrets are murmured, whispered like cheers.
A glade bathed in silver, with moss underfoot,
Fairy fireflies twinkle, as if they were soot.

Ancient trees listen, their branches entwined,
Guardians of stories, both gentle and kind.
With secrets concealed, and mysteries spun,
Every leaf holds a truth, under the sun.

By the flickering shadows, a magic unfolds,
Tales rich and vibrant, in silence they hold.
With starlit guidance, the night softly bleeds,
Into stories of wonder, where imagination leads.

So wander the glade with an open-eyed heart,
For secrets awaken when darkness imparts.
A symphony swirls as the constellations sigh,
In the starlit embrace, dreaming never says goodbye.

The night will embrace you, with whispers of fate,
In the glade's gentle arms, where miracles wait.
Through the shadows of magic, in peace you'll reside,
For secrets of the glade are forever your guide.

Whimsy in the Foliage

In the lush green forest, where dreams take their form,
Whimsy is hidden, in every norm.
Leaves twinkle with laughter, a soft gentle cheer,
While creatures of magic draw ever so near.

A rabbit in a waistcoat, with tales to unfold,
Rambles through the ferns, each story retold.
The breeze carries giggles from high in the trees,
As dappled sunlight winks, with playful ease.

Beneath floral arches, secrets entwine,
Every petal a treasure, a path to divine.
The foliage dances in whims of delight,
As shadows play tag with the warmth of the light.

Let your spirit meander, through the soft greens and gold,

For every leaf whispers, its secrets behold.
In the hush of the glen, where magic takes sway,
Whimsy is waiting, to color your day.

So skip with the breezes, and twirl with the sap,
In the heart of the forest, take a moment to nap.
For in whimsy and wonder, your heart will ignite,
In the foliage's embrace, all dreams feel just right.

Threads of Enchantment

In a tapestry woven tight,
Threads of magic dance in light.
Softly whispered spells take flight,
Glimmering dreams in the dead of night.

Colors blend, both bold and shy,
Woven tales of the earth and sky.
Each stitch a story, a secret, a sigh,
Where the heart of the enchantress lies.

Moonlit shadows weave their song,
Echoes whispering all night long.
In the charm where we belong,
Threads of enchantment, wild and strong.

Elders speak of ancient lore,
In each knot, a cherished core.
The web of wonder, forevermore,
Enfolds us in a quiet roar.

So let us dance 'neath starlit skies,
Feel the magic as it flies.
With open hearts and hopeful eyes,
We'll craft our tales as daylight dies.

Whispers Beneath the Canopy

Beneath the trees, a soft embrace,
Whispers linger, time and space.
Leaves murmur secrets, a gentle trace,
In the heart of the forest's grace.

Sunbeams filter, golden and bright,
Dancing shadows in the fading light.
Nature's symphony, pure delight,
Sings of magic within our sight.

Mossy carpets where fairies tread,
Ancient paths where dreams are led.
Feel the pulse in the spirits' thread,
In the sanctuary where hopes are spread.

Softly gliding on the breeze,
A tale unfolds with every tease.
In this realm, the heart finds ease,
As nature whispers, inviting peace.

So linger here, where wonders dwell,
In every whisper, a story to tell.
Embrace the magic, the wild spell,
Beneath the canopy, all is well.

Secrets of the Silken Night

In the hush of the evening's hue,
Secrets glisten, deep and true.
Stars twinkle like dreams anew,
As the silken night enchants the view.

Veils of mystery drift and sway,
Silent shadows guide the way.
With every breath, the night will play,
And weave its tales where starlight lay.

The moon, a lantern high above,
Bathes the world in tender love.
Unseen whispers from skies above,
Wrap the night in a velvet glove.

Come ye wanderers, heed the call,
In the dark, we shall not fall.
For within the night, we find our all,
The secrets shared, the moonlight's thrall.

So let the night knit our dreams tight,
As we wander where shadows invite.
In the tapestry of stars so bright,
We'll unveil the secrets of the night.

Starlit Silhouettes on Hidden Paths

On paths where moonlight casts its glow,
Starlit silhouettes dance to and fro.
In whispered tales of long ago,
Secrets of dreams begin to flow.

Twilight's canvas, a jeweled veil,
Guides our footsteps with a sailor's trail.
In the hush of night, we set sail,
With stories afloat, our hearts won't fail.

Branches weave like fingers wide,
Cradling shadows where mysteries hide.
Every corner, a tale to bide,
In the gentle night, our hopes abide.

As we wander down these paths unseen,
A flicker of magic in between.
Connecting hearts where dreams convene,
Starlit silhouettes, a tranquil scene.

So follow the whispers, heed the sounds,
In the quiet magic that surrounds.
With starlit silhouettes, our joy abounds,
On hidden paths where love astounds.

Whispers of the Moonlit Cloth

In shadows spun from silver threads,
The moonlight weaves its secret tales,
As whispers dance in midnight's grasp,
And silence hums where magic prevails.

Beneath the stars, old stories sigh,
Each stitch a memory, soft and bright,
In fabric worn by time's caress,
A tapestry of dreams takes flight.

Through gentle folds, the past unfolds,
A journey carved in each delicate seam,
In twilight's song, the heart is bold,
As threads entwine in a woven dream.

The fabric shimmers with a soft glow,
Entwined with laughter, echoing years,
Each whisper spun in twilight's thread,
A quilt of hope amidst our fears.

So listen closely, dear wanderer,
In every stitch a secret rhyme,
The moonlit cloth will sing to you,
A timeless tale beyond all time.

Secrets in the Twilight Stitch

In twilight's hush, the needle glides,
With secrets stitched in threads of gold,
Each loop conceals a world within,
Where dreams and wonders softly unfold.

The fabric sighs with faded tales,
Of laughter lost and shadows cast,
In every corner, mysteries dwell,
Of cherished moments from the past.

As twilight deepens, shadows blend,
The stitches pulse with hidden grace,
Unraveling echoes of the night,
A woven dance, a timeless place.

With every pull, each knot secured,
The whispers of the night take flight,
In patterns drawn by moonlit hands,
A tapestry spun from pure delight.

So hold it close, this twilight cloth,
Embrace the secrets gathered here,
For in each stitch, a heart can glean,
The whispers of a night held dear.

Enchanted Threads and Starry Dreams

In starlit skies, the threads entwine,
A dance of hope through midnight's veil,
With every stitch, new dreams align,
Where magic sings and shadows pale.

Each fabric glows with secrets bright,
As wishes whispered on the breeze,
In patterns bold, the heart takes flight,
Across the night, amidst the trees.

The needle pierces with gentle grace,
Stitching together realms unseen,
Where every loop conceals a place,
A world alive with vibrant sheen.

With enchanted threads, we weave the night,
A canvas rich with tales we share,
In every color, joy takes flight,
A patchwork quilt of dreams laid bare.

So let your heart be stitched with light,
And let your spirit twirl and gleam,
For in the fabric of the night,
We find our hopes and starry dreams.

Beneath the Goblin's Gaze

In shadows deep, where goblins dwell,
Their watchful eyes like lanterns glow,
With mischief spun in every tale,
They guard the secrets earth bestows.

Beneath their gaze, the night unfolds,
A tapestry of dark delights,
With every flicker, curiosity swells,
As magic dances through the nights.

Their laughter echoes in the gloom,
In hidden nooks, where treasures lie,
With mischief threaded in the loom,
As whispers weave through starlit sky.

Each stitch a promise, every seam,
Crafted by hands of cheeky sprites,
With goblin's glee and playful scheme,
The fabric brims with wild invites.

So dare to glance, beneath their gaze,
For every thread holds tales anew,
In goblin's world, in shadowed maze,
Discover magic waiting for you.

Caps of Gossamer Dreams

In twilight's hush, the shadows creep,
Whispers soft, the secrets keep.
A shimmer glows on mushroom's crown,
In this enchanted, moonlit town.

Dreams woven in a silken thread,
With starlit wishes, hopes are fed.
Gossamer caps, in colors bold,
Guard stories of the young and old.

Underneath the ivy's veil,
Lies a path where fairies sail.
Through emerald leaves, the magic swells,
In midnight's arms, the wonder dwells.

Catch the breath of sparkling dew,
With every step, imagine new.
Capricious winds begin to sing,
Of dreams alive in fanciful spring.

So wear your dreams, let none take flight,
Upon those caps, through endless night.
For in each thread, a tale awaits,
Of gossamer dreams and hidden fates.

The Secret Stitches of the Fae

In shadows deep, where fairies weave,
The secret stitches, none perceive.
With needle bright and thread of light,
They sew the stars that guard the night.

Tiny fingers, nimble and quick,
Crafting wonders, magical trick.
Each patch a tale, each knot a sigh,
Beneath the moon, where wishes fly.

Dancing softly on blades of grass,
The fae's laughter, like rippling glass.
Their work is woven with love and care,
Stitches spun from the evening air.

Wings adorned with colors rare,
In secrets shared, a bond to bear.
Threadbare paths of shimmering seams,
Hold the heart of forgotten dreams.

As dawn approaches, they bid goodbye,
But in each stitch, their legends lie.
For in the fabric of dusk and morn,
The fae's magic is forever worn.

Enigmatic Wares of the Woodland

In hidden glades, where shadows play,
Strange wares await at break of day.
Amber drops and leafy charms,
Enchanting treasures wrapped in arms.

A foxglove bell, so softly rings,
While ancient trees keep watch on things.
Glimmers of gold in twilight's grasp,
In woodland corners, secrets clasp.

With every glance, a story grows,
Of clever sprites and whispered vows.
Whimsical trinkets, lost and found,
In nature's bounty, magic's bound.

Petals soft as a lover's sigh,
With each token, a heartfelt cry.
In the arcane woods, where shadows roam,
Enigmatic wares call us all home.

So venture forth, where dreams unfold,
In every trinket, a tale retold.
Woodland whispers to open ears,
Invite the laughter, drown the fears.

Aurora Caps and Forest Tales

As dawn awakens with ribbons bright,
Aurora caps drink in the light.
Colors swirled, from dawn to dusk,
Nature's palette, vibrant and husk.

In corners hidden, tales are spun,
Of forests deep and races run.
With every breeze, the stories sway,
In whispered song, through night and day.

Beneath the boughs, where shadows glide,
Adventurous spirits, filled with pride.
Chasing echoes of laughter near,
In every step, we conquer fear.

The sun sets low, the shadows play,
A tapestry of night and day.
Where dreams take form in sylvan halls,
And echo softly as twilight calls.

So gather 'round, both young and old,
In tales of warmth, let hearts unfold.
For in the forest, truths prevail,
Through aurora caps and forest tales.

Midnight Adornments and Fairy Lores

In the hush of night, stars shimmer bright,
Dreams take flight beneath the moon's soft light.
Fairies dance in shadows, laughter in the breeze,
Whispering secrets, as they weave through trees.

With jeweled crowns and wings of gossamer,
They bless the timid heart, a gentle traveler.
In the glow of dusk, their magic unfolds,
Tales of love and wonder quietly told.

Each petal glistens, bewitched by night's embrace,
A wonderland where time dares to lose its pace.
Crickets serenade, as silk threads unite,
Midnight adornments, a mesmerizing sight.

They gather forgotten wishes, softly spun,
Transforming starlight into threads of fun.
With laughter echoing in the still of the day,
Fairy lores we cherish, lighting our way.

In moonlit flurries, as dreams intertwine,
We find the magic in moments divine.
So let the whispers carry you beyond,
To a world where enchantment is never foregone.

Hats Woven with Wishes

Beneath the sun's warm glow, a hat takes shape,
Crafted by hands that weave dreams without escape.
Each stitch a promise, each thread a desire,
A whimsical wonder, setting hearts afire.

With ribbons of laughter, and colors of glee,
These hats tell stories of who we can be.
Mapping journeys on the fabric of the mind,
In each tiny fiber, a treasure to find.

From the peaks of the mountains to the depths of the sea,
A hat woven with wishes as magical as can be.
Adventurers don them, with hope in their eyes,
Awaiting the wonders, the vast, open skies.

Each hat holds the dreams of those who dare,
To chase after sunlight, to wander and share.
Through valleys of laughter or storms that might brew,
Woven with wishes, they'll carry us through.

So place it upon your head with delight,
Let it guide you forth into day and night.
For in each gentle weave, you'll find a way,
To embrace every moment, come what may.

Echoes of the Elven Canopy

In the heart of the woods, where whispers reside,
Elven laughter dances, a spirited guide.
Through emerald canopies where sunlight dips low,
Echoes of magic in the twilight glow.

Branches weave tales of old, rich and bright,
A tapestry woven, both mystical and light.
From the depths of the roots to the tips of the leaves,
Ancient secrets whispered in the warm summer eves.

With each fleeting breeze, a story takes flight,
And shadows are stirred, igniting the night.
Elven songs float in the stillness so pure,
Calling the dreamers to rest and to allure.

They speak of the stars, of lost worlds anew,
Of the paths untraveled, of hopes that ring true.
In the echoes of laughter, we find our own song,
In the heart of the woods, we finally belong.

So tread lightly and listen, let your spirit roam,
Through the echoing whispers, you'll find a home.
For the magic of elves in the canopy high,
Awaits every seeker with dreams in their eye.

The Fabric of Whimsy and Wonder

In a realm of enchantment, where daydreams reside,
The fabric of whimsy is stitched with pride.
Soft as the clouds, vibrant as a song,
Interwoven tales where we all can belong.

With threads of imagination, and needles of light,
We weave our own destinies, chasing the night.
Each patch a memory, a dream that we share,
In the quilt of our lives, love lingers in the air.

Dancing with colors that shimmer and sway,
The fabric invites us to laugh and to play.
From the fabric of wonder, our stories take flight,
Guided by starlight, our souls feel the light.

So gather your dreams, let them unfurl,
In the tapestry spun, your magic will whirl.
For in every stitch, there's a chance to redefine,
The fabric of whimsy is yours and is mine.

With each thread, weave a tale of your own,
For the heart finds its rhythm when gently it's sewn.
In the fabric of wonder, there lies sweet reprieve,
So dance in the magic, and boldly believe.

Elven Shadows and Fabric Dreams

In twilight's glow, the shadows play,
Where whispers weave in soft ballet.
Elven shadows dance on leaves,
As moonlight spills and softly cleaves.

With fabric dreams that stretch so far,
They stitch the night with silver stars.
A tapestry of secrets spun,
In every thread, the past is won.

Gentle hands of fate and time,
Crafting tales in whispered rhyme.
Where silence cloaks the forest deep,
And echoes of the night do seep.

Each twinkling light, a story told,
In velvet hues of dusk and gold.
A realm where all is possible,
Where hearts and dreams are tangible.

So let the shadows guide your way,
Through fabric dreams that softly sway.
For in this world of mystic blight,
Elven shadows weave the night.

The Velvet Crescent Beckons

Beneath the sky's deep velvet shade,
A crescent moon begins to wade.
With glowing gaze, it softly calls,
To wondrous lands beyond the walls.

The stars emerge like scattered seeds,
To nourish dreams where longing leads.
Each sparkle holds a secret sigh,
As night embraces those who fly.

In whispers felt on breezes light,
The velvet crescent claims the night.
It beckons hearts both bold and shy,
To reach for dreams that seem awry.

With every breath, the essence swells,
In magic's grasp, the spirit dwells.
A tapestry of hopes unfurled,
Where wishes dance in starlit world.

So follow, dear, where shadows drift,
The velvet crescent is a gift.
In night's embrace, let spirits soar,
For magic waits on dreamer's shore.

Enchanted Threads of Twilight

As twilight weaves its silken spell,
In hues of lavender, deep and swell.
Enchanted threads of dreams take flight,
In whispers soft as falling night.

The stars emerge with flickers bright,
A guiding light in fading night.
Each thread, a tale of joys and tears,
In the loom of time, it softly steers.

With nimble fingers, fate entwines,
The fabric of the heart's designs.
Amidst the echoes of the past,
A tapestry of shadows cast.

Within the twilight's gentle hold,
Each woven dream, a story told.
In every corner, magic gleams,
Entwined in all our hidden dreams.

So cherish well the threads we find,
As twilight whispers, hearts aligned.
For in our lives, the magic streams,
An endless dance of woven dreams.

Forest Echoes and Starlit Whimsy

In forest deep, where shadows creep,
Echoes call from silence deep.
A starlit whimsy fills the air,
With laughter light and gentle care.

The trees, they sway with ancient grace,
In secret glades, a hidden place.
Where whispers roam on winds that play,
And time dissolves like misty spray.

With every rustling leaf that falls,
A melody of nature's calls.
Each step a journey yet unknown,
In forest's heart, we're never alone.

The stars above, like lanterns bright,
Illuminate the velvet night.
With every glance, the wonders gleam,
In starlit woods, we dare to dream.

So heed the whispers, soft and clear,
For forest echoes draw us near.
In starlit whimsy, let us find,
The magic woven through the mind.

Fables of Foliage and Fabric

In the deep woods, leaves dance bright,
Threads of gold in soft twilight.
Whispers speak through branches high,
Tales of magic as they sigh.

Mossy carpets hold secrets vast,
Stitching time, the shadows cast.
Nature's loom weaves tales so clear,
Fables told for those who hear.

Fluttering wings of emerald hue,
Stitched with wonder, dreams renew.
Every petal, every seam,
Threads of life in twilight's gleam.

The forest breathes, a living page,
Each creature writes from age to age.
Crickets hum their gentle tune,
Underneath the watchful moon.

Beneath the boughs, where stories blend,
Fabric of life will never end.
In each rustling leaf and laugh,
Lies the heart of foliage's craft.

The Curious Creations of Moonlit Fascination

Under the moon's soft, silver glow,
Curious shadows swirl and flow.
Wonders crafted, delicate and fine,
In the stillness, they intertwine.

Glimmering dreams hang from each star,
Whispers of worlds both near and far.
Night unfolds its velvet arms,
Cradling secrets, voicing charms.

The nightingale sings in twilight's hush,
Your heart races in the soft blush.
Mysteries twirl in the moonbeams' flare,
Enchanting souls with magic rare.

Fancies flutter like lantern light,
Guiding lost hearts through velvet night.
Curled in shadows, wonder stays,
In the stillness of whispered ways.

Collect the dreams, they patch the skies,
Every secret, whispered sighs.
In the tapestry of night's embrace,
Find your truth in the lunar space.

Woven Whispers in Elven Ears

In the glade where moonlight weaves,
Whispers linger among the leaves.
Elves listen close to tales of old,
In their hearts, the stories hold.

Threads of starlight, softly spun,
Awakening magic with every run.
Voices flutter through the night air,
Casting spells with tangled care.

Gentle stories whisper low,
Of ancient trees and lovers' glow.
Every sigh, a promise deep,
In Elven dreams, they gently seep.

Laughter rings like silver bells,
Echoing in enchanted spells.
Woven tightly, the fables sing,
In the hearts of those who cling.

Elven ears hear the unseen,
In every glance, a glimpse of green.
Through woven whispers, truth unfolds,
In the tapestry of night, it holds.

Gossamer Veils in the Heart of the Grove

In the grove where shadows play,
Gossamer veils keep doubt at bay.
Softly swaying, delicate threads,
Enfolding dreams where silence treads.

Beneath the boughs, a sacred space,
Where whispers brush, and doubts erase.
Every moment wrapped in light,
In the magic of the night.

Deers wander through the misty sheen,
Where nature's charm is clearly seen.
Each heartbeat thumps with life anew,
With the secrets of the dew.

Gossamer dreams float in the air,
Carried softly, without a care.
The heart of the grove hums a tune,
A harmonious dance beneath the moon.

In every veil, a story lies,
A treasure map for wandering eyes.
Quiet magic, gentle and slow,
In the heart of the grove, they flow.